Sabine Picout

Various Book, Theater and Film Reviews

Nick Hornby, Charles Dickens, Peter Shaffer, Tolkien, Phil Penningroth

GRIN Verlag

Bibliografische Information der Deutschen Nationalbibliothek:

Die Deutsche Bibliothek verzeichnet diese Publikation in der Deutschen National-
bibliografie; detaillierte bibliografische Daten sind im Internet über http://dnb.d-
nb.de/ abrufbar.

Imprint:

Copyright © 2004 GRIN Verlag GmbH
Druck und Bindung: Books on Demand GmbH, Norderstedt Germany
ISBN: 978-3-656-32686-1

This book at GRIN:

http://www.grin.com/en/e-book/205673/various-book-theater-and-film-reviews

Leopold-Franzens-Universität Innsbruck
Institut für Translationswissenschaft

Reviews

vorgelegt von:

Picout Sabine

Innsbruck, am 2003 - 2004

Table of Contents

I. Book Reviews

(1)   Nick Hornby's High Fidelity

In Nick Hornby's first novel *High Fidelity* the main character, Rob Fleming, recounts in flashbacks his "most memorable split-ups"[1], and so the reader is taken into some troublesome periods of the protagonist's childhood and adolescence. Rob reflects on his various relationships and tries to find reasons why they have failed. Then the action shifts into the present and the central character can be accompanied during the most recent months of his life, just after his girlfriend, Laura, has left him and moved in with Ian - the man who lived upstairs. Although at first Rob is not sure whether to be distraught or relieved, he is later convinced that he wants Laura back again and can't stop calling her.

In the meantime he dates the singer Marie LaSalle, who makes him cry with her cover version of "Baby, I Love Your Way", but it's probably only because he thinks it is great to sleep "with someone who had a recording contract"[2]. At this time Rob also tries to meet up with his previous girlfriends again.

A short time after Laura has moved her stuff out of Rob's flat, her father dies. The reunion with his girlfriend takes place at the funeral of Laura's father, after which Laura asks Rob to sleep with her. But Rob is worried that she has had unprotected sex with Ian and that's why they only go to a pub to talk. He feels that he doesn't "need to offer to become a different person: it has happened already."[3]

The plot of the novel is set in the 1990s and refers to the political atmosphere of the early 1990s in Britain which is "one of quiet deflation after the exuberant economic and consumer attitudes of the 1980s"[4].

In *High Fidelity* the main protagonist of the novel tells about his life in a way that the reader could assume that it is a confession by this 35-year-old man. As the novel is written from the perspective of Rob Fleming, it is told in the first person.

---

[1] Hornby, Nich: High Fidelity. Penguin Books, London, 1995, p.1
[2] ibid, p. 103
[3] ibid, p. 184
[4] Knowles, Joanne: Nick Hornby's *High Fidelity.* The Continuum International Publishing Group Inc, New York, 2002, p. 32

Rob's whole life has revolved around music and classifying it into top five lists. (The top five Elvis Costello hits, the top five episodes of Cheers, the five best side one tracks of all time. He is unable to rank music according to more important criteria. It is significant for Rob's character that, just after Laura's abandoning him, he reorganizes his record collection. He often does this during periods of emotional stress and he likes "the feeling of security" he gets from his "new filing system"[5].

Nevertheless, after Laura has left Rob, he wakes in the night, reflecting on his life:" I'm here, in this stupid little flat, on my own, and I'm 35 years old, and I own a tiny failing business, and my friends don't seem to be friends…" and he is " in danger of falling off the edge."[6] Depressed, he reminisces about his life with Laura, the last woman he was living with, who had even got pregnant and lost her child when he had a brief affair with another woman.
The author shows how Rob tries to find a meaning to his life and how he undergoes a process of moral and spiritual maturing.

Rob is not a hero; on the contrary, he represents an everyman character who characterizes himself as "average"[7], who needs someone "who can stop "him "from falling down into the pit where the permanently single live with their mums and dads" because "lonely people are the bitterest of …all"[8]. Laura decides to bring out Rob's "potential as a human being."[9]

In my opinion, it is very uncertain that the relationship will be satisfying and successful because Laura realizes that Rob is not a soulmate and I suppose she can only put up with this because at that moment she is too tired to banish him out of her life.

I think what makes the book so fascinating is that it describes real life. People and situations the narration is dealing with are down to earth and could correspond to true life and it discusses matters that everybody experiences. Nick Hornby's style is fascinating, full of wit and charm.

[5] Hornby, Nick: High Fidelity, p. 44
[6] ibid, p. 36
[7] ibid, p. 27
[8] ibid, p. 117
[9] ibid, p. 202

(2)   *Charles Dickens' Christmas Carol*

One foggy Christmas Eve, Ebenezer Scrooge returns from his office to his cold empty house. There his long-dead business partner Jacob Marley appears before him, moaning about the miserable state he is in because of his meanness when he was still alive. He tries to warn his old partner that having neglected his fellow men he will also end up the same way. He is told that three spirits will offer him a salvating chance.

First, the Ghost of Christmas Past takes him back into his childhood. When his boyhood and youth appear before him his heart of stone melts. He realises that his master had great sympathy with the less wealthy and that he was treated very humanely by him.

Afterwards the Ghost of Christmas Present shows him the misery of his relatives and the difficult life of his assistant, Bob Crachit.

Lastly the Ghost of Christmas Yet To Come explains that if he does not change his way of life he will die lonely and he will be mourned by no one. From this time onwards the wealthy businessman lives a better life. He begins giving generously to charity and celebrates Christmas contentedly.

Ebenezer Scrooge, the tight-fisted old man, is the epitome of avarice. The wealthy businessman is entirely without pity for the poor and without any friends. His only aim in life is making money and he gives absolutely nothing away to the less fortunate. He pays his poor assistant a very low wage and treats him very strictly and without any mercy.

His former business partner, Jacob Marley, had the same greedy and grasping character. That's why his ghost has been forced to wander the world, wearing a heavy chain. Seven years after his death he returns to haunt Scrooge in order to prevent him from similar tornaments.

For Bob Crachit and his family life is difficult. Nevertheless they are cheerful and happy, because they have always been satisfied with what they have. Even the youngest son, who is sick and lame remains merry and pleasant. The boy's life can only be saved if he is helped by Scrooge. Bob is very subservient and although he is aware of the injustice of his boss he is not rebellious in anyway. He even comes to Scrooge's defence when his wife complains about the way he is treated.

This book strikes the reader as a fairy tale, it portrays the British bourgeoisie of the nineteenth century when industrialization was growing rapidly.

The author, Charles Dickens, paints a realistic picture of the poverty of the working class and the ignorance of the political system at that time. He manages to capture the mood and atmosphere of his time perfectly by describing the daily routine of working class people, their housing and their habits. He mentions the poorhouses of the poorest people as well as the excessive eating and general merriment of the wealthier. This way Dickens succeeds in contrasting those two worlds and he manages to stress the miserable living conditions of the working class.

A passage that is really touching or even shocking is when Scrooge says of the poor, "If they would rather die...they had better to do so, and decrease the surplus population.".

Such radical views typify the unfeeling attitude and behaviour of many people who had grown rich and who were obsessed with money during the boom of Britain's economy in this period of industrialization. Many of them were as selfish as Scrooge and did not want to share their wealth with the poor and homeless.

By describing the horrendous living conditions of those poor people the author tried to put the government under pressure to undertake social reforms and he wanted to tell the rich to keep their preoccupation with money in check.

The reader finds it particularly easy to believe in the picture Dickens gives of life in Britain and therefore he had already in his time succeeded in maintaining liberal opinions.

Dickens knows perfectly how to keep his readers in suspense. The terrifying vision of the moment when Scrooge sees the face of his dead partner staring straight at him is certainly impressing. With the help of his vivid and variable but purposeful descriptive style the writer really makes his characters appear in the mind's eye of the readers."...the dying flame leaped up, as though it cried, "I know him!..." ...His body was transparent: so that Scrooge, observing him, and looking through him, and looking through his waistcoat, could see the two buttons on the back of his coat ..." The reader really sees the deathly-cold glazed eyes staring at him. The characters of his novel are full of "normal" people without any flamboyant features and qualities who nevertheless do not bore us. The fact that he describes common life is one of the reasons why Dickens has become so popular.

II.   Theater Reviews

(1)   Peter Shaffer's Amadeus

Peter Shaffer's *Amadeus* was first performed at the National Theatre in London in 1979 and won London's major drama prizes. A revised version opened in Washington (1980) and a month later it was heading for Broadway, where it was finally awarded with five Tonies.

The play concerns an allegory about the rivalry between Antonio Salieri and Wolfgang Amadeus Mozart and it examines the possibility that Salieri, the court composer to Emperor Joseph II of Austria, has poisoned the youthful genius musician Amadeus Mozart.

The play meets the aging composer in the hours before his death when he tells the audience in flashbacks about the career of his divinely gifted contemporary. In his youth Salieri makes a bargain with God: in order to earn lasting fame as a composer, he promises to glorify God by making his music. When the younger and much more talented Mozart arrives in Vienna, Salieri is confronted with the limits of his own musical gifts and his mediocrity and can no longer suppress his jealousy because he realizes that he is no match for the excellent creativity and artistic imagination of the much younger artist. Salieri's hatred makes him rail against God's injustice and destroy Mozart's life.

Although the action revolves around Mozart and his musical excellence, the artist's rival Antonio Salieri is the play's central character. It's fantastic how Götz Burger, portraying the old and mentally deranged composer, who addresses the audience directly as "Ghosts of the Future" is able to slide from old age to young years just by applying a few simple gestures, such as putting on some hairgel.

By his amazing and dazzling vocal technique the actor manages to enact different- sometimes lengthy - stages of Salieri's life without interrupting the flow of the play.

Mozart's character (Gerhard Kasal), a turnoff, a boorish sometimes even obscene and giggling infantile child prodigy, is perfectly portrayed. The way this talented actor manages to interpret the challenging role of the free-spirited and joyful temperament of Salieri's rival earns considerable applause for his acting.

The scene when Constance (Sinikka Schubert), Mozart's wife, comes with her son at the very last instant to her husband's deathbed and, when the boy is embracing his dying father, is really impressive. At this moment the audience are offered an incisive insight into the personality of genuine artists. This heartbreaking scene shows the tragedy of Mozart, whose life has been destroyed by the malicious plot of his adversary, a man blinded by hatred.

A brilliant production under the assured direction of Hans Escher, which can be highly recommended.

III. Film Review:

(1)   Tolkien's The Fellowship of the Ring

The film is adapted from Tolkien's work *The Fellowship of the Ring*, which is the first part of his trilogy *The Lord of the Rings*. With the series of books the author tried to compensate the lack of a typical English mythology.

Tolkien's central concept of the quest of the ring has remarkable precedents like "*The Ring of the Nibelungen*" and "*Arthur's Legends*", all of which have already been converted to the big screen.

Up to now nobody else other than Peter Jackson has dared to transform Tolkien's fantastic legend into film. With his screen adaptation of "The Fellowship of the Ring" Peter Jackson was not only a pioneer, but he has gone far beyond what all the others before him have achieved.

The "Fellowship of the Ring" takes place a long time ago in a mythical land called Middle Earth.

In the centre of the action are hobbits, human-like creatures, who are small and docile, with furry feet. They inhabit the Shire, an imaginary country and they live in burrows.

One of these hobbits, Frodo Baggins (Elijah Wood) is the hero of the film. His Uncle Bilbo (Ian Holm) had an adventure 60 years before and came back with a strange ring that allowed the wearer to disappear from view. It also granted the power to rule and to dominate other people:
"*It is the "one" ring to rule them all.*"

At the beginning of the story, Bilbo celebrates his "eleventy-first" birthday. He wants to retire and therefore he chooses Frodo to be the bearer of the ring. The sensitive and intelligent nephew of Bilbo must protect the ring from Sauron (Sala Baker), the evil king of Mordor, who had forged the ring centuries ago and then lost it. Sauron, the representative of Evil, has most of the other rings and now wants this one to possess all power.

Gandalf (Ian McKellen), an all-knowing wizard, realizes that the hobbits will play a great part in saving the world from the evil powers. He knows that Sauron and his nine black riders want to get back the powerful ring. He makes a plan to prevent the ring from falling into the wrong hands, and first sends Frodo and his friend Sam (Sean Astin) to carry the ring into the realm of the elves. From Riverdell, Frodo must carry the Ring to Mount Doom and throw it into the volcanic fires.

Now the fellowship for the ring forms. It comprises four hobbits - Frodo, Sam, Pippin (Billy Boyd) and Merry (Dominic Monaghan) - the mysterious man called Strider, Aragorn (Viggo Mortensen) - the rightful king, Boromir (Sean Bean), the elf Legolas (Orlando Bloom), the dwarf Gimli (John Ryse-Davies) and of course the wizard Gandalf.

As the title indicates, the mission can only be fulfilled because of the loyalty of Frodo's fellows. Their journey is filled with dangers; there are attacks from strange black-cloaked riders; they are beset by forces of evil in the forms of nature. The fellows go through incredible experiences, hardships and pains in order to survive. They even experience the deaths of Gandalf and Boromir before Frodo and Sam strike off on their own. Pippin and Merry are captured by Orcs. Aragon, Legolas and the dwarf set off to rescue them.

The Fellowship is a beautifully told fable of our times, behind which lies the idea of life being a quest and an unending struggle between good and bad.

It is a magnificent overall performance and the director has with great imagination succeeded in constructing a fantastic world of "fairy-tales", with elves, dwarfs and trolls. He has also brought cultures like those of the dwarfs and the elves to real life. The quest leads the audience through fascinating imaginary worlds and beautiful landscapes, which lend colour perfectly to the psychological states of the hero and his companions and helps in revealing their characters. The figure of Sam, the totally loyal friend, serves from time to time as a clever vehicle for comic relief.

The actors manage to build up an atmosphere full of suspense not least because of perfectly mastered computer special effects and tricks. Very impressive is the performance of Elijah Wood's staring Frodo, the hobbit who inherited the magic ring.

Peter Jackson has converted Tolkien's classic theme in a most convincing way for the cinema. It's understandable that the film is a huge success and has achieved cult status, especially amongst younger viewers.

(2) *Phil Penningroth's "Silence of the heart"*

The film "Silence of the heart" by Phil Penningroth is about the suicide of a teenager. It describes the isolation and the depression of the 17-year old Skip, who is not very self-confident. He is a failure at school and cannot achieve his aims.

In addition to this there is not a lot of confidence between Skip and his parents because he can't talk about his problems to either his mother or to his father. He wants to be loved by them but feels unwanted.

We get the impression that he does not feel happy with his family because they are nagging him, especially his father, who keeps reminding him to work harder, to make more effort. But he cannot live up to their expectations.

Even in his relationship to girls Skip does not have much success. He falls in love with an older girl, Andrea. But she rejects his feelings. She is a rather superficial girl and does not suit him. She does not take him seriously.

At the same time Skip does not realise that Penny, a girl he has known for a long time, has deeper feelings for him and he is not aware of how much she really likes him. She understands Skip and suffers because he hardly takes any notice of her and he does not reciprocate her feelings towards him. He thinks of her as a real "friend" and for him the thought of her being his girl-friend seems impossible.

Skip is rejected by his peers and even his friend Ken can't help him. Perhaps this is because on the one hand he is not mature enough and on the other hand - as we get to know at the end of the film – he does not feel comfortable within himself. Although he seems to have no material problems he suffers from his mum's emotionally cold attitude.

Just before dying Skip asks Ken if he would announce his own suicide to his friend. I was very much affected by this episode. Ken does not take these remarks in earnest and responds by telling him that he will not do it because he does not want to burden his friend with such a responsibility. At this point the viewer becomes aware of the role that the environment usually plays in cases of suicide.

This scene shows us and makes us realise how easy it is to get into a situation like this every day and that the person in distress should be able to rely on us and that we should give the needed and longed for support.

Skip becomes despondent when no one seems to understand - or love - him. His death at first looks like an accident. But his younger sister Cindy, with whom he had had a lot of disagreements, starts putting things together. She is the first one to discover how much Skip had tried to reach out to friends and family for reassurance and had found none. She regrets having had so many conflicts with her brother and can't hardly get over this fact. But later she is able to see through Skip's peculiar behaviour and she understands a possible suicide did by this boy.

When the parents are invited to the student counsellor to talk about the suicide, Skip's father reacts angrily and does not feel comfortable in this situation. He can't face up to the truth and gives the impression of being rather weak. He feels like a criminal and is totally wrapped up in self reproaches. But when he looks back he remembers situations where he did not understand various hints his son had given him.. He feels guilty because his son could not share his feelings with him and because he hardly ever found reassuring words for him.

Skip's mother is able to face the facts much sooner and she realises that she made a lot of mistakes and that she did not show enough emotional concern. She goes to see Penny, who makes it clear to her how much pain Skip had been in. Later this experience enables her however to prevent another suicide – that of Ken.

Towards the end, when Skip's mother stands on the edge of the cliffs and tells Ken, who wants to kill himself, "It's better to live" – is really touching and moved me to tears.

After Skip's death all his friends and the members of his family are ashamed and do not want to take their share of the responsibility although they know that the guilt is spread around in equal quantity. All the survivors feel a lot of regret about the suicide.

As the title indicates the boy's heart became silent and died because the hearts of all the others he loved and appreciated remained dumb. None of them replied to his questions or listened to his wishes and nobody paid any attention to his cries for help. He committed suicide because he thought that there was no other solution to his problems. His depression and hopelessness had made life seem unbearable.

Perhaps the film wants to teach us a lesson, to be more sensitive and more sympathetic with those who live around us. That's how everybody (who was close to the adolescent) could have been aware of at least one of several warning signs and they could have taken his allusions seriously. Although the film was produced in the early eighties its topic is still timely and the way the problems are dealt with is not less effective.

This theme touches a lot of people, above all adolescents as in our time the pressures of society are increasing, relationships become more and more superficial and nobody takes care of his fellow human beings. Therefore feelings like hopelessness, despair, self-doubt and world weariness increase and ever more often become unendurable.